Open Wounds
By Kori Jane

To my mother,
with whom I share
my tears, my laughs, and my pencil.
I treasure you dearly.

"Love isn't soft, like the poets say.
Love has teeth which bite and the wounds never close."

Stephen King

Contents

Heart

-

"You do not yet suffer enough to suit me."

Friedrick Nietzsche

Funeral

and I was bleeding for *you*
I was cutting away my skin
down to the bone
I was removing and changing
and decorating and eliminating
sculpting myself into someone you could love
and it worked didn't it
you didn't notice I was dying
you didn't even notice I was bleeding
you were too mesmerized by my eyes
to see the tears they were shedding
you didn't see the knife I was holding
had slowly started making its way to my throat
you were my date to the funeral
of the girl I used to be
and I cried and I let you hold me
and when my funeral was held
you realized you didn't know how to grieve me
you didn't know that version of me at all
and in order to resurrect my identity
I had to leave you
I wonder if it makes you sad
that the girl you kissed in the back of your car
doesn't exist anymore

you didn't see the blood
you were too in love
and I lost who I was
all so I could be somebody you could love

I love so hard it looks like violence
I fight so hard it looks like love

Claustrophobia

Sometimes you have to leave your lover
because they love you too much.

You loved me so much you became me
and I became you.
We were so close we converged.
You tried getting closer and closer
until you went through me.
We were facing back to back.
"Turn around!" you screamed.
But by then we were miles apart.
Half of me remaining.
You kept the part of me I liked.
All that was left was you.
A few years later
I saw you at the grocery store.
I asked you to give me myself back.
But I was stuck to your bones.

Sometimes you have to leave your lover
because they love you too much.

Playing Pretend

I think I could love you the girl said
to the boy she had crafted in her head.
For the one in front of her looked nothing of him,
but the beautiful girl had already dived right in.

I think I could love you she murmurs again.
He shakes his head but plays pretend.
*How do you love someone you barely know? H*e questions.
Unaware of how quickly she births new obsessions.

Whatever you say the boy whispers, rubbing her back,
knowing she will flee once she sees all he lacks.
She melts under the superficial touch of another,
plotting how she'll turn this boy into a lover.

Artist

He was an artist.
I was his muse.
His fingertips painted me
in red, yellow, and blue.
I let him glue me to a canvas.
I hung up there for centuries.
As long as he kept looking
I didn't mind living just to look pretty.

The Other Woman

"You are the other woman!"
Her friends press.

"I know."
She whispers.

"Do you not feel bad?"
They ask.

"Of course I do. But sometimes feeling desired
is stronger than the guilt. For a moment at least.
It doesn't make it right. It just makes it complicated."
She says, putting on her makeup.

"He is using you!"
Her friends press.

"I know."
She whispers.

"Do you not care?"
They ask.

"Of course I do. But sometimes being used feels better
than not being wanted at all. For a moment at least.
It doesn't make it true. It just makes it complicated."
She says, grabbing her keys.

"He'll break your heart!"
Her friends press.

"I know."
She whispers.

"Don't you hate heartbreak?"
They ask.

"Of course I do. But sometimes when your heart
skips a beat you forget the inevitable. For a moment at least.
It doesn't make it wise. It just makes it complicated."
She says, shutting the door.

Claw Marks

She scratches his arms with her gentle fingertips.
He wakes up one day with claw marks on his skin.
She holds his hands with her soft palms
while cold handcuffs begin to rust around his wrists.

Dust

I think
the trees understand me
more than you do. The way they
bend and grow without saying a word.
I got so tall and bore so many leaves. I grew so much
you had shrunken to the size of a pea. So small you fit in my
pocket. I was silent while you yelled at me as if I could
stop it. Do I take the blame for growing up
towards the heavens while you
stayed the same? Am I to
climb down
to the
ground
because
you could
not catch
up? Is it
my job
to get
on your
level
just so
you are
not left
in the
dust?

Kori Jane

Unrequited Love

the only reason
I still believe in love
is because of the way
I love others

equally returned love seems unattainable
when the love you give is often immeasurable

I am his good friend.
He is my obsession.
I would bleed for him.

He would clean up the mess.
Instead of asking me
who caused this distress.

Kori Jane

Forbidden Fruit

You planted in me a tree
from which sprouted the forbidden fruit.
You picked an apple
and we ate every bite
till we reached the core.
Make me drunk with poison
So we may forget our sin.

Shots

He was a few drinks in
an hour before the sunset began.
The beautiful boy told me I was beautiful,
through slurred words,
yet it still sounded meaningful.
A week into January,
broken his goal for the new year.
He tried to kiss me,
a breath full of beer,
but I pulled away.
He'd forget this the very next day.
We talked of our families,
hopes, dreams, and scary things.
And I listened close.
I only hear his heart when his livers lost hope.
I don't spend much on alcohol,
I don't like to feel out of control.
But your body
is a bottle of cheap tequila
so pour me a sip from your mouth.
I can be a drunk for you.
Give me some of your pain,
I'll wear it proudly too.
Let me sober you up,
I know what to do.
Although I can't save you
from sinking in booze
when you love the way it feels to be drowning.
How can I win someone over
who likes to lose?
Funny how you love me most
when you aren't sober.
How am I to be a hero
when I don't know the real you?
Which boy am I saving,
The atheist from Saturday night,
or the boy on Sunday praying?
Which one of those two loves me?
If I save you from this sea of liquor
will you look at this girl in front of you
and not even remember?

Kori Jane

Can I keep taking shots for a boy
who takes too many shots to see
the bullet wounds for him
I wear on my skin?
How can I tell someone
death is worth escaping,
When he is living in a grave
of his own making?

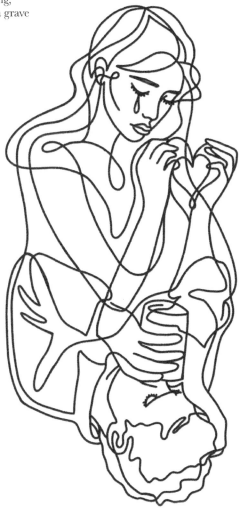

.

What some call codependence others call love.
What some call healthy others call indifference.

You Love How You Drive

You picked me up in your car.
It was without blemish.
Shined, scrubbed, vacuumed.
I could see the reflection of my car
in your rearview mirror as we pulled away.
Smudges of dirt. Chipped paint.
Dents from years gone by.
Why then was I surprised
when you did not come back
the next night?

You love how you drive,
and something that clean
has something to hide.

Is my inability to break
from harmful relationships
innocence or apathy?
The line between
naivety and masochism
is less of a line
and more of an arrow.

Burning

you watched the movie
while I was watching you

you looked at the sky
while I was looking at you

you stared at the fire
while I was staring at you

you had time to flee from the flames
while I was burning watching you run

When Love Becomes God

The girl was in love.
The boy was in devotion.
When she looked into his eyes
she was filled with adoration.
A summer love type affection.
When he looked into her eyes
he was filled with hungry acceleration.
A forget who you are addiction.
He put her on a pedestal falling to his knees.
He was worshiping someone
who could never meet his needs.
She was so far up, his hand out of reach.
He told her God made them for each other
and then he made a church out of her body.
A temple out of her mind. She was his god.
And he was simply her lover.

As they inevitably part
he's healed from codependence
while she's left with a broken heart.
She asked if they could stay together.
He shook his head and off he fled.
Although she did nothing wrong
she can't help but feel shame hearing their song.
But it's not her fault she reminded him
of a past self he hated so much.
He's sorry not to come around anymore.
It's not her fault he stopped calling.
She balanced things with such ease
it was hard to understand why he had to leave.
But it was not his fault he was falling.
Stuck between pleasure and purpose,
he had to choose his calling.

Like They Are You

you left so quickly
I had no preparation
no plan on how
I was to dispose of the love
I saved for you
so it never left my hands
I try to find a place for it
shoving it down the throat of others
until they choke on it

I love every boy like they are you
I wonder if they don't stay
for the same reason you went away

if only I wrestled with relationships
like I wrestle with religion
the less romance I see
the more quick I am to wonder
if God really loves me

Perfect

"We are so perfect together," The boy said.
She asked him to prove it.
He grabbed her hand and cut out some of the veins,
shaved down the knuckles that were in the way.
He intertwined their fingers,
"See how well we fit together," he said.
She nodded as blood dripped onto her legs.
"I love you," the boy said.
She asked him to prove it.
He began to kiss her bleeding thumbs
and then her lips.
The blood from her broken skin stained her mouth.
He pulled out a mirror,
"See how pretty you look with red lips" he said.
She admired the beauty he brought out in her
and mourned her stolen identity.
He bandaged her wounds.
She thought he was sweet.
She'd lost too much of herself to remember
it was he who caused this bloody surrender.
"We are so perfect together," the boy said.

> A statement she now believed
> for the girl she used to be was dead.

Pomegranates

Do you remember our conversation about pomegranates?
I love the act of peeling them more than I love the bitter taste.
They take time and care to prepare.
You have to be gentle when cutting one.
Peel back patiently to avoid missing one of its gems.

You had never tried one before.
It had seemed like too much work.
I began to cut you one. You took the knife from my hands.
Insisting you could do it yourself. You butchered it.
The skin went everywhere, juice staining the floor.

When I asked if you liked it, you nodded.
But you said you wouldn't peel one again.
It was too much work, you would rather eat an apple instead.
I think you viewed me this way.
You liked my taste but I was too much work.

You made me believe I was too hard to love.
I know now that isn't the case.
You just wanted love to be easy.
You wanted to pick up those pre-plucked pomegranate seeds,
you didn't care if they came covered in preservatives.

You thought peeling away a woman's clothing
would lead you to the beautiful fruit.
You didn't like that I had more layers to peel away.
I handed you the knife and held out my arms, ready to bleed.
But I wasn't worth the mess.

I would peel a million pomegranates for you.
But it wouldn't have mattered.
You would have just complained
about the way the juice left stains around your lips.
Instead of thanking me for opening it.

Will you love me the way Adam loved Eve,
sacrifice a rib so I may breathe?

His Facade

his voice was so gentle
she didn't see the filth
pouring out his mouth as he spoke
    until it was on her hands

his touch was so tender
she didn't see how his fingers
where breaking her skin
    until she felt the wounds

his eyes were so kind
she didn't see them
undressing her in his mind
    until her clothes were on his floor

his lips were so sweet
she didn't see them leave cavities
on her teeth as he kissed her
    until the poison sealed her mouth

his words were so soft
she didn't see how they hurt her ears
with every phrase he whispered
    until the sound was deafening

he walked with steps so quiet
she didn't hear the footsteps
as he was leaving
    until he was already gone

Do it Right!

but if you are going to leave me
do it RIGHT!

watch the bits and pieces of my body you once read like brail
blow onto your handsome face as you point the trigger
   don't put me out of my misery
     let me bleed out slowly

         if I can't experience love
        I suppose the euphoria of death
       is the closest intensity to obsession

and when you stab me in the back
       TWIST THE BLADE

let me scream in pain
   with you behind me
     as to not remember
       how beautiful you looked
        standing in front of me

She hated herself more than she loved him.
She hated herself so much he started to hate her too.

Hunting

The boy I love
likes to hunt.
I ask him
to pursue me.
Shoot me dead
as long as it means
my head will lay
next to the deer above his bed.

Drowning

I should've left while we were drowning in love
it would have been better to die
sinking in blankets and co-dependence
then the alternative

we swam back up to the top for air
pulled the plug letting the water drain
until we were stuck at the bottom
of an empty lake we once flooded

I wish we parted ways
because we were drowning
not from dehydration
as we watched our love drain

what is summer without passion
what is winter without love
is summer just hot
and winter just cold
without someone to swim beside
without someone to hold

Kori Jane

New Door

And they always come back
Once you've healed and moved on
They knock on your door
No matter how you've decorated and changed and grown
No matter the new color you've painted the wood
To rid all memory of him
He knows where your door is
And he will tell you "It looks different. *You* look different."
And you will think to yourself how you do not feel different
Every distraction you crafted to forget him
Has left *you* as the unrecognizable one
Yet he recognizes you and he comes back
And you let him in
Not because you love him but because you miss being loved
Although it does not feel like it did
Lovesick without the love

And you will write a poem about it only to realize
You loved writing
More than you loved writing to him
And you loved loving more than you loved him
And no matter how much time may pass
You will let him in when he comes back

    And you start to watch the paint chip
    And you wonder if it was beautiful
    Before or after he opened it

I could be a martyr for my religion.
If God is love,
I could die for love.

Brain

-

*"You laugh like a little girl,
and inside you think like a martyr."*

Fyodor Dostoevsky

I'm Not Okay

People flock, in need of words.
I always know just what to say.
I bandage their deepest hurts
when sadness gets in the way.
Out to dinner with friends
I bow my head to pray.
But alone inside my room
my God, I do not obey.
I'm good at helping others
especially through dismay.
But I'm no good person.
Shame threatens soul decay.
Born to understand others
show them another way.
Myself never understood
Never asked if I'm okay.

Strong Woman

they call me a strong woman
they call it a gift
I walk through the door
and people turn to hear me speak
but I desperately wish
I did not suck up so much air
to comfortably breath
I want to be small
I want to fit into the hands of those I love
instead of carrying their bodies on my back
I want to be soft not severe
I am not fragile enough
to be worthy of handling with care
don't call me a strong woman
for the stronger I seem
the weaker I feel

I clothed myself
in overabundant serenity
for fear of being seen
as something they could hurt
I used to hang up my armor before bed
let my skin breathe when no one was around
but it won't come off anymore
up all night poked and prodded
trapped underneath expectations
thrown on someone *strong enough to take it*
I'm longing for someone to break it
someone who sees me as worthy
of handling with care
a soft woman needing repair
after confusing the word strength
with the word despair

i am my mother's defender
and my father's daughter.

my mother's sadness
and my father's apathy
are at war in my mind.
their battle wounds
i confuse as mine.

i used to think
i was the white flag
that would cause a surrender
but i am another soldier.

fighting for the desire
to be heard
above her cries
and above his silence.

over the screams
i cannot say a word.

if there is no audience
to perform for
what does that make me
      lonely or authentic

WHO AM I WHEN I AM NOT PERFORMING

Stone

what is one to do
when they have a positive disposition
and a chronically guilty conscience

when I yell for help
my smile etched in stone
forbids the screams from coming out

is the act of living
supposed to make me feel like a villain
I think my guilty conscious is broken

Sea

There once was a little girl raised by monsters.
A father with talons for arms and daggers for nails
and a mother with fangs for teeth and slits for lips.
Both with silver horns and skin of red scales.

She did not know anything else.
So her long silky hair and soft blue eyes
her kindness and sweet smile she believed
made her the one to despise.

They attempted to shape her into one of them.
When it failed she was thrown to the street.
Suddenly seeing others like herself, she had to flee.
She needed her monsters to feel complete.

A lovely girl when surrounded by unpleasantry
counts *her* beauty as hideous.
Others tried to take her in
but she couldn't accept love unless it was insidious.

-the girl who grew up drowning finally had a chance to breathe
but fresh air was unfamiliar so she floated out to sea

Kori Jane

being a teenage girl
is not unlike being a grown woman
the rules are roughly the same
don't be too ugly or you won't fit in
don't be too pretty or you'll outshine your friends
ignore your heart
but wear it on your sleeve
dress to impress
unless you are walking the streets alone
flirt enough to get him hooked
but never let him take you home

i get into bed
stay awake
make up for time i wasted
thinking about wasting time
why in those hours
do i miss my bed
while i lay in it

Kori Jane

A Letter to the Monster Under My Bed:

As a little girl, I made you angry.
Never scared of you when I was a child.
Never asked my dad to check for you under the frame.
Never cried to my mom when you lurked in the dark.
I perplexed you. I was supposed to be terrified.
You wanted my innocence devoured.
I mistook you for a friend.
Talked about my life with one who meant to make me cry.
Never giving you the rush of invoking fear, so you left.
I stopped believing in imaginary friends quickly after.
Never big on playing pretend on the playground,
or waiting up for Santa I knew wasn't coming around.

Is this why you haunt me now that I am grown?
Why you still keep me awake at night?
Sending my way those I will mistake for friends
knowing I will give my heart to them.
I still confuse you.
For although you make me tear,
you still do not make me scared. I have you figured out.
Since I never gave you a place to live under my bed,
you moved in with all the demons in my head.

Hungover

I drank so many people's tears as a child,
I am perpetually hungover.
Absorbed the grief from my parents,
and their parents' parents, until I was falling over.

My friends go to the bar to numb their pain,
but I empty liquor down the sink.
Searching for someone else who will pour
their miserable sadness into my drink.

Longing to fill an existential thirst.
My troubled soul runs dry.
Without the presence of another's suffering
I crave being the shoulder on which to cry.

I drank so many people's tears as a child,
I am perpetually hungover.
I feel too deep. I think too much.
Will I ever from pain be sober?

Beach

My friends and I drove down to the beach.
I watched their silhouettes run into the water.
I was sprawled out on the sand.
I hate the feeling of it between my toes.
dirty didn't always mean ugly, did it?
The sand was messy.
It reminded me of growing up.
Their bodies under the moonlight
fell beneath the crashing waves.
Before they shot back up they let themselves taste
what it's like to be submerged.
In that moment I don't see them
I pray the Texas heat melts them into the water.
So they wash up onto the shore.
I could put them in a bottle.
I've made a habit of making myself small,
I know I could crawl inside
then we could all stay there together.

I want to stop growing up
so I can start living

Space In Between

I only know how to survive between two extremes.
The walls of vice and virtue are closing in.
The only thing worse than living in darkness instead of light
is lurking in the hallway in between.
Bright enough from the crack in the door
to see where the darkness leads.
Dim enough to hide behind this disguise.
A girl who bounces between numbness and neurosis.
Between psychosis and silence,
obsession and indifference,
anxiety and apathy.
In Sunday School they said Satan was evil.
But they never taught me how beautiful she looks
dancing in the space
between loneliness and lovesickness.
Oscillating between spiraling and stillness,
excess and emptiness.

Kori Jane

my life is a balancing act
trying to mend all pain
with the very things
that caused it

Anxiety Angel

Anxiety makes me feel like a child
who has done something bad or wrong.
The world singing in unison
while I hum a different song.
Never convicted, always guilty,
Anxiety hides behind beautiful pearls.
Constantly awake in my mind
in her innocent sun dress she twirls.
Blaming the 'devil' on my shoulder,
she says "he's the darkness, I'm the light."
She lives to silence his voice
from sunrise through the dead of night.
With this pressure unending
the 'devil' warns I'll end up dead,
while Anxiety insists I need to be perfect.
They continuously wrestle in my head.
He tells me to block her out.
That I am good. That I am kind.
But how do I perform a lobotomy
on my terminally restless mind?
Anxiety disguises as an angel
but she is far from friends with God.
A wolf dressed in sheep's clothing.
Which of us is the biggest fraud?
She crushed my tender conscience.
Guilt now searing through my veins.
Having bloomed inside of me
billows of hurt and pounds of shame.
Could this 'devil' she calls my adversary
accused of making me slip,
be what's left of the real me
desperately trying to escape her grip?

> *Who else knows me completely?*
> *Would I even exist without my anxiety?*

58

I used to think
this sadness in me,
made me kind.

But I think
it has just made me
unlovable.

Mother Nature

I never believed
I was a product of Mother Nature,
rather a child of God.
But man, did God make,
like weather,
my mother's nature.
Joy like the beaming sun.
Anger like the roaring sea.
Kindness like a subtle breeze.
Sadness like hail.
Strength like an unwavering tree.
But ever-changing
like the forecast tends to be.
My mother grew up
loving lighting and thunder.
For me, grey skies over blue,
I've always been fonder.
My mother's nature confuses chaos with calm
so I'd rather sink in the rain
then bask in the sun.
I think my mother and Mother Nature
would be good friends.
Creating mountains with breathtaking views.
While digging the deepest of valleys.
I watch as a daughter is prone to do.
Praying for the next drop
of water from the sky
so I can blame the weather
not my mother's nature
for making me cry.
Is a daughter's nature nothing
if not the same as her mother's
mother's mother?
All the way back to Eve.
In a garden with perfect sunshine
yet she still chose to leave.

Kori Jane

loneliness

loneliness lives in silent empty parking lots
it lives in the invisible cracks of bedroom walls
it lives in the bare alleyways of deserted towns

but loneliness also lives in packed places
it lives in the doorways of parties
calling me to stand alone in the back searching for an exit
it lives in the candles of birthday cakes
calling me to question if these people singing know me at all
it lives between the spaces of words shared between friends
calling me to realize I have outgrown all of them

loneliness does not depend
on the number of people you have around
loneliness is a feeling of isolation
a lack of belonging
that can't be cured by the existence of a crowd

Soul

-

*"I am so pathetically intense.
I just can't be any other way."*

Sylvia Plath

Kori Jane

i do not lick my wounds i wear them like armor

i do not taste my guilt
i chew until it turns into shame

i do not swallow my grief i let it come out
in the silence between my words
for there is no more room for it in my mouth

Nothing Matters

"nothing matters" I say with tears in my eyes,
my head in my hands.
"nothing matters" you repeat with a smile,
nodding in satisfaction.

"nothing matters"
I feel my body empty as it leaves my lips.
I cry because
I want to feel fulfilled.

"nothing matters"
You feel your body empty as it leaves your lips.
You smile because
you have nothing to worry about inside.

Is this why
we do not belong together?
You hear my thoughts as if
they are said with your intention.

We say the same words; we mean the same thing.
We both empty as it leaves our lips.
But you get a sense of relief
while I am overcome with dread.

> *- I seek significance*
> *while you seek simplicity*

Kori Jane

something about grief
makes a child lose faith in fantasy

Depression

She grew up hearing depression
trapped people in bed.
Growing up she avoided her bedroom
concluding depression was not her battle.
Undiagnosed yet medicated.
She used parties as prescriptions
people as pills
substances as psychologists
chaos as a way to silence her thoughts.
She prided herself on being busy.
Her calendar full. Her soul empty.
But in the moments alone she knew
depression was eating her brain.
She couldn't make it go away
so she fed it whatever she could.
Stuffing herself with plans and drinks.
And friends and social media.
Satisfying depression with overindulgence.
If only she'd have learned
depression does not have a human appetite.
The more it is fed the more it wants.
Always hungry but never full.

Depression had devoured all that she loved.
When she was alone, it was all she was made of.

Last Night

"I cried myself to sleep last night."

"I'm sorry."

"Don't be. I feel like myself again."

"Is this a good thing or a bad thing?"

"I'm still trying to decide."

Open Wounds

August 17th 2003
    the day I was born
August 17th 2003
     somewhere in the world
     a tree was planted
She is 20 years old

I wonder if she knows I've been growing alongside her
I wonder if her branches bend in accordance with my limbs
    does she reflect my outsides or insides
    short in stature or tall like my dreams

dragged down by the weight of the leaves she won't shed
clinging to them through winter or she would feel naked
stripped away from the ones who depend on her to survive
    when woodpeckers come to taste her sap
    do beaks get stuck in her honey-colored blood

do new rings appear with each tattoo inked into my skin
with every bruise I collect does she begin to rot
has she been overwatered by my ever-flowing tears
does my tree pick at her imperfect bark to look prettier
    (or is that something only I do
    when looking in the mirror)

does the touch of another cause her to decay
    as others
        climb and step
            or crush and saw

I run to thunder instead of seeking shelter
    did the storms
        I danced in
           kill my tree

       Is this why there is a longing inside of me?

Kori Jane

Inner Child

Do things for your *inner child* they say.
But I don't remember her.
Under all this hard exterior,
she must be locked away.
She was only a girl when I stole the stage.
Behind the label of *old soul* she would hide.
I thought being mature was a game.
And I was determined to win.
How am I to heal my *inner child?*
When I never let her out.
I shut her eyes and plugged her ears.
Clamped my hand over her mouth.
I didn't know growing up so young,
would hurt me in turn.
How did I go from the crib to 20?
What happened in between?
Is that all faded memory?
A childhood buried in burdens,
no one intended for me to carry.

Kori Jane

In another universe my grandmother is still alive.
She plays me Jack Johnson and I am at peace.

I was born with wings instead of feet.
Always needing somewhere to flee.
Across state lines and oceans. Airplanes and highways.
No destination in mind. Just a need to run away.
I want to go home but I don't know where that is.
Certainly not the place I lived as a kid.
I was too trapped by my own humanity.
I want heaven. I want to escape all this tragedy.
I fly up to the gates but the angels laugh.
And God looks down at me with much love and much wrath.
Did I really think I would be let in before my time?

I am the daughter of Icarus.
    Confusing my fleshly wings with the wings of angels.

Always

always tired never sleep
always hungry never eat
always bored never outside
always questioning never know why
always praying never listen
always a vice never addiction
always writing never heard
always an afterthought never preferred
always sad never cry
always anxious never shy
always driving never home
always lonely never alone
always guilty never good
always oversharing never understood
always longing never fulfilled
always angry never kill
always scrolling never offline
always an angel never divine
always in the mirror never pleased
always attached never leave
always smile never frown
always a leader never a crown
always Shakespeare never Juliet
always used never kept
always a flirt never a whore
always seeking never find more
always an old soul never a child
always a prude never wild
always at fault never blame
always sorry never change

I do not want to be fed
chocolate covered strawberries
on a picnic blanket.
I want someone to feed my misery.

- my sadness is hungry

Kori Jane

I Don't Know How to Walk Anymore

I was told to cherish my childhood.
That I'd grow up in the blink of an eye.
But I didn't listen. I ran to each birthday.
Quickly blew out the candles.
I never believed I'd reach adulthood.
I ran and ran full speed ahead until my feet gave out.

I sit on the grass to rest. I look at my hands.
They are older. I am 20.
I don't know where my childhood went.
I try to run back. But everyone is passing me by.
The world keeps spinning in fast motion while I'm frozen.
At the gates of childhood pleading to be let back in.
I watch my younger self running towards the door.
I yell at her to slow down but she can't hear me.

I will keep running until my legs fall clean off.
I'll fall back on the grass. Look at my hands.
See wrinkles forming. I will be 30.
And I will wonder what I did with my 20s.
I will run towards the 20s gate and beg to be let back in.
I can hear her now. She tells me to slow down.

But I don't know how to walk anymore.

End of the World

and as God decides it's time for the world to end
bodies turn to dust and it's time for souls to ascend
my guilt in chains have me bound
as angels lift me from the ground
"you must be so relieved" the angels say
grabbing my arms to take me away
I fight to stay with my feet on the grass
"relieved" I ask
"wasn't it good, wasn't it fun" I hear from everyone
am I the only person who still needs to get things done
on earth I never really felt at home
but once my time was up I stayed on earth alone
I went to every house of every person I'd ever loved
I remember standing there hands covered in blood
"I'm sorry" I shout
but it didn't matter they are all gone now

Kori Jane

I am terribly good at cutting ties.
I think instead of fingers I was born with knives.

Kori Jane

my name is Kori Jane
　　　(my parents picked it out)
　　　　　Kori is a boy's name
　　　　　　　(but the Jane made it soft)

my mom just calls me Kori now
I grew up and outgrew the pretty part
so people forget about the Jane
　　　(they forget I am soft)

I've gained a lot of followers and lost a lot of friends
I used to think I was extroverted but now I want to stay in
I like to spend time cooking
　　　cutting onions reminds me
　　　　　I like crying more than laughing

I have always loved thunderstorms and reading stories
　　　books that make my tears blend in with the rain
　　　　　reminds me of the porch where my father spends
　　　　　　　Sunday mornings drinking coffee
　　　　　　　(I wish he painted more)

my favorite color is brown
I was never a fan of things brighter than my dreams
when I was little I never wanted to grow up
but now I wish I could stay the same
I want to see the world before Jesus takes me home
I want to lay in my childhood bed and feel like I am home
I look for those who are hurting so I can bandage them up

I put people on pedestals
　　　Maybe if they view me from up above
　　　　they will see that I am small
　　　　see that I am soft

　　(and remember I like to be called Kori Jane)

I have a longing inside of me.
An earnest hunger I cannot satisfy.
I've spent most of my life looking
for someone who will help me search.
But the closest I've come
are people who yell
so loudly they silence it.

Garden

when i was little
i ate a sunflower seed
so flowers would grow inside of me
i cut open holes in my skin
so the sun can get through
i cry streams of tears
so they have water to drink
i let people speak filth into my mouth
so they have enough dirt underneath

my body may be falling apart
but at least I have a garden in my stomach

Kori Jane

You Missed It

you slept in
and you missed it
the noise stopped
but you didn't notice
you went to sleep late
to escape your misery
and you missed it
but the noise stopped
your head stopped spinning
your heart stopped beating
your skin stopped bleeding
your eyes stopped crying
and the noise stopped
but you missed it
and you woke up
and you saw
that everyone else
had grown up
as if overnight
they found
the secret to life
and you were asleep for it
and the noise was loud
and you couldn't think
you didn't realize
all you needed
was to wake up
but you sleep away the healing
and you stay up long enough
to feel the hurting
and you missed it
but the noise did stop
while the world kept turning

Hands

-

*"I put my heart and my soul into my work
and have lost my mind in the process."*

Vincent van Gogh

Fraud of a Poet

I wish I was better at making love sound beautiful.
Some call me a poet, but I call myself a fraud.

Can I write about my heart fluttering
without reaching my hand inside my throat
and placing my arteries on the page?
Can I write about a lingering touch
that leaves goosebumps on my skin
without those bumps turning into bruises?
Can I write about a time
butterflies danced in my stomach
without throwing up on the paper?

I cannot write about beauty
without it sounding a little ugly.
I cannot write about ugliness
without it sounding a little beautiful.
I cannot separate what is fantasy
from what is real.
I cannot love an angel
without remembering
the devil was once one too.

Yellow Paint

Van Gogh used to eat yellow paint.
Attempting to consume
a happiness the color exuded.
A stomach of darkness
he desired to be painted in a color so vibrant.
One of the most talented of his time
yet he cut off his ear.
Maybe to silence the demons in his head.
His paintings lasted longer
then his life he ended himself.
His last words *"sadness will last forever."*
His very best work
done in a mental institution.
He pulled the trigger in a field of sunflowers.
Maybe to be surrounded
by the color he wished to have inside.

I used to hate my depression.
I used to medicate my anxiety.
Now I let it be.
I don't feed it. I let it feed me.
I use the tears I was born crying
to create that which others find inspiring.
It seems those given the gift of creativity
will always live a life swimming in melancholy.
We can choose not to drown in it,
not by trying to drain it away.
But by using the water
to make something worth remembering.
I have come to appreciate the parts of me
that others find crazy.
So they may find sanity
in the art my crazy expels from me.

Kori Jane

To Love a Poet

"You have no idea the love letters
I could have written to you."

"I know you could have filled up
every journal in the world
but that doesn't mean I like to read."

Mason Jars

i was little when i learned
they liked my sadness
when it was a performance
i was little when i learned
i was good with my words but bad with my feelings
the adults in my life told me i could make it big
there was something in my tears others wanted to drink
they began to watch me with mason jars in their hands
every time my tears fell
they would rush up to me
catching drops in the glasses
they sold them for pennies
quenching their thirst by chugging my vulnerability
thus having no tears left to cry for when i was thirsty
they did not know how to take my sadness seriously
unless I dressed my pain up in beautiful imagery
giving them stacks of stories
wrapped in poetic similes
they clapped and cried
and sold them for fives
i was little when i learned an artist's pain is only addressed
as entertainment distracting others from their own distress
if not picked and prodded into something they could buy
would they even care to acknowledge my unwritten cries
they say roll up my pain
stuff it in paper to make
a blunt with my blues
light it with a pencil
and smoke it until beautiful stanzas are exhaled from my lips
they tell me my problems are pretty when written on a page
i was little when i learned i was ugly unless dressed in words
i was little when i learned i need a microphone to be heard
i was little when i learned
my sadness must be palatable
or they will choke on my tears
that are too heavy to swallow

writing poem after poem
about people who love my writing
more than they love me

Never

I am never the protagonist
in someone's story.
Never the antagonist.
Never the white knight.
Never the damsel in distress.
I know my job.
I am the writer.
I don't belong in fairytales.
I create them.

'

Kori Jane

Some hide behind their tear-soaked tissues.
But mine are piled high in a stack,
thick enough to write a book.
Maybe profit from all I lack.

Born with open wounds
that never heal.
I feel everything intensely.
Always compulsion.
Never indifference.
Even emptiness is heavy.

Black ink pours
from these open wounds.
But I never dull an ounce
of this misery
for when my eyes are dry
so is my pen.

books close open wounds

Body

-

"She never looked nice. She looked like art,
and art wasn't supposed to look nice;
it was supposed to make you feel something."

Charles Bukowski

Kori Jane

use me for my words
use me for my smile
use me for my heart
use me for my eyes

use me for something i am proud of
something i can stand the looks of
but you insist on using the thing i despise
you wish to use my skin and ignore my mind

I am good!
I yell pounding dents into my chest
and though you never questioned my morality
I just need someone to agree
so I may put my fists to rest
your head fits so nicely
laying on the car-sized impression in my flesh

in wanting so badly
to be kind and to be nice
I ruined myself in the process
but if I'm good enough for you
I'm good enough for something
I must be good
or all this hurt counts for nothing

Kori Jane

you take a piece of me as you leave
and *I* apologize for how
my severed body bleeds
on your clothes
that are clean because of me

Red

Her lips tasted of love, lemonade, and wintergreen.
His lips tasted of hunger, liquor, and nicotine.

Her veins once flowing with two things:
one part blood
one part innocence.
Lust poured out of his mouth as he kissed her.
His lust didn't replace her innocence.
Like oil and water
they did not mix well.
Lust and innocence gave birth to shame.

Her lips tasted of desire, bubblegum, and Carmex.
His lips tasted of swear words, Miller Lite, and easy sex.

Her veins now composed of four things:
one part blood,
one part innocence,
one part lust,
and one part shame.

Her lips tasted of softness, lipstick, and candy.
His lips tasted of aggression, cigarettes, and brandy.

Her hands once clean
now were stained.
Her lips, once sweet,
now tasted of his sweat.
Her blood once flowing blue
is now gushing red.

Her lips tasted of innocence, blood, and shame.
His lips tasted of lust, sweat, and her name.

Dead Woman

how many bodies
must you be buried beneath
before you are too dead to care
that you are just a corpse to them

how many times will you make a mess
in the name of making love

Kori Jane

I tell myself it's not my fault
that I confuse stranglings with hugs
but I know the truth
I don't know how to separate
pleasure from pain
need from love

but when does one reach womanhood?
is it the day they bleed as they lose their first egg
or when they lose their virginity?
what is girlhood if not a loss of blood?
is it really womanhood
if you don't feel a part of you is dying?
someone has killed the girl she once was.
the blood is on her hands
on her legs
on the seat
of his car.

Emptiness

Will you show me there is wholeness
in this emptiness you've created?
I asked you to fill this longing
but you have only made it bigger.
Now I'm wrapped around your finger.
At least I'm wrapped around
something besides my knees.
Eyes on something else aside from a phone.
Although your eyes are foreign to me.
Will I ever find a place I feel at home?

'

I am so soft people don't know how to love me.
Too much touch and I melt into an absence of identity.
Too little touch and I start to harden.
I fit in the palm of people's hands.
I slip between their fingers instead of holding them.

Spirit

-

"The fact that our heart yearns for something Earth can't supply is proof that Heaven must be our home."

C.S Lewis

Kori Jane

It wasn't that God was silent,
I knew He was speaking.
It wasn't that the world was silent,
I knew there was noise.
For even the sky when it rains
is groaning with all of creation.
It wasn't an inability to hear God.
It was an inability to hear anything.
My mind had gone deaf.

It rained today.
I could not hear the drops.
I stretched out my hands to feel them
and found it was *my* fingers clogging my ears.

Adam and Eve

Adam, this question I press:
which one felt emptier,
the promises to you the snake did attest,
or the gaping hole that was left
after your lover took the rib from your chest?

Eve, this question I frame:
which one felt heavier,
the forbidden apple or the relentless shame,
or was it the broken chains
when your Creator called you by name?

Talking to God

"God, why is it so hard to be good?
Oh, how desperately I want to be good."

"If you were able to be perfectly good,
why would you need me?"

Cross

Jesus was a carpenter.
When he was strung on a cross
did he splinter against wood
he carved as a boy?
When they pressed nails into his hands
did he think of the nails
he hammered as a boy?
When he began to bleed
did he taste the wine
we drink on Sundays?
Did the smell of the wood
remind him of his humanity?
"My God, my God,
why have you forsaken me?"
He cried out.
Was this an echo of all creation?
Is it such a surprise
he died on a piece of wood?
Material made from a tree.
The very thing in the garden
that led to his sacrifice.

Kori Jane

and the difference between
the haze from the smoke machines on worship sundays
and the smoke from her weed
is one goes into the lungs
while one goes in one ear and out the other
      are the bruises on her knees
      from kneeling at the pews or from being used

and the difference between
her guilt from drinking communion wine
and her guilt from drinking the bottle in her kitchen
is that one's from feeling she doesn't deserve a drink
and one's from drinking too much
      are the absent calories she doesn't taste
      from fasting for the Lord or wanting a smaller waist
         uneaten broken bread over which she forgets to pray
         (unless she's worried about being saved)

and the difference between
her bible and her body
is that the book is untouched
and the latter is covered in handprints
and she wishes it was the other way around
      are the tears that she is crying
      from losing God or loving him

and the difference between
her beliefs and Satan's
is that while they both acknowledge God exists
one is cursed
and one is forgiven
      are her mistakes not evidence
      of God's mercy and grace
         is this duality of her humanity
         not just further proof of her need to be saved

Kori Jane

Mirage

when I was little I hated Eve
it didn't seem fair to me
just because one person was deceived
now my life is something I grieve

I do not hate her anymore
I wonder if when she looks down from heaven
her heart feels a familiar sore
watching me hate the parts she shamefully bore

if it were me and my pride
after a snake whispered beautiful things in my ear
to my Creator I too would have lied
to this very day from him I still hide

I wish to see an image of God
when I look at my reflection
but all I see is a mirage
a glorious being on the face of a fraud

Are We All Just Puppets to God?

Sometimes I feel like God's puppet.
His glorious fingers holding my eyes open
using strings made out of angel wings
to lift me up from bed each morning
just to throw me to the ground.

Sometimes I feel God breaks and bends
just so he may have something to mend.
Have I endured all of this misery
just so he may feel accomplished in my story?
Me a mere test subject of faithfulness.

But if this were truly true,
him the puppet master and me his muse,
why would he be allowing these doubts?
For pain can't be something he gladly allows
but rather for opening eyes to see what he saves us from.

I have strings leading to heaven.
I cut them and tie them around my throat.
Until he gently unravels the knots.
Not so he may have something to fix
but so I feel his presence fully assured he does exist.

Kori Jane

I wrote in the margins of my Bible
God why do you ignore all my pain?
I imagined God sitting in heaven and laughing,
for I was asking in pen on his tongue
if he even had a mouth.

"Do you take pride in your hurt?
Does it make you seem large and tragic? Well, think about it.
Maybe you're playing a part on a great stage
with only yourself as an audience."

John Steinbeck

Kori Jane Spaulding, a 20-year-old author from Houston, Texas, has garnered acclaim for her debut poetry collection, "Books Close." As a rising voice in contemporary poetry, Kori Jane's sequel poetry collection, "Open Wounds" marks the beginning of her literary journey as she prepares to branch into novel writing.

Made in the USA
Las Vegas, NV
12 July 2024